When the
DARKNESS

BOOKS BY JOHN PIPER

God's Passion for His Glory
The Pleasures of God
Desiring God
The Dangerous Duty of Delight
Future Grace
A Hunger for God
Let the Nations Be Glad!
A Godward Life
Pierced by the Word
Seeing and Savoring Jesus Christ
The Legacy of Sovereign Joy
The Hidden Smile of God
The Roots of Endurance
The Misery of Job and the Mercy of God
The Innkeeper
The Prodigal's Sister
Recovering Biblical Manhood and Womanhood
What's the Difference?
The Justification of God
Counted Righteous in Christ
Brothers, We Are Not Professionals
The Supremacy of God in Preaching
Beyond the Bounds
Don't Waste Your Life
The Passion of Jesus Christ
Life as a Vapor
A God-Entranced Vision of All Things
When I Don't Desire God
Sex and the Supremacy of Christ
Taste and See
Fifty Reasons Why Jesus Came to Die
God Is the Gospel
Contending for Our All
What Jesus Demands from the World

When the DARKNESS Will Not Lift

Doing What We Can
While We Wait for God–and Joy

JOHN PIPER

CROSSWAY BOOKS
WHEATON, ILLINOIS

When the Darkness Will Not Lift: Doing What We Can While We Wait for God—and Joy

Copyright © 2006 by Desiring God Foundation

Published by Crossway Books
         a publishing ministry of Good News Publishers
         1300 Crescent Street
         Wheaton, Illinois 60187

Cover design: Josh Dennis

Cover photo: iStock

First printing 2007

Printed in the United States of America

Scripture quotations marked ESV are from the ESV® Bible (*The Holy Bible, English Standard Version®*), copyright © 2001 by Crossway Bibles, a publishing ministry of Good News Publishers. Used by permission. All rights reserved.

All emphases in Scripture quotations have been added by the author unless otherwise noted.

Library of Congress Cataloging-in-Publication Data
Piper, John, 1946–
When the darkness will not lift : doing what we can while we wait for God and joy / John Piper.
    p. cm.
    Includes bibliographical references.
    ISBN 13: 978-1-58134-876-7 (tpb)
    ISBN 10: 1-58134-876-2
    1. Depressed persons—Religious life. 2. Spiritual life—Christianity. 3. Expectation (Psychology)—Religious aspects—Christianity. 4. Trust in God. 5. Patience—Religious aspects—Christianity. 6. Depression, Mental—Religious aspects—Christianity. I. Title.
BV4910.34.P57   2006
248.8'6—dc22   2006026383

VP		18	17	16	15	14	13	12	11	10	09
16	15	14	13	12	11	10	9	8	7	6	5

To the memory of
JOHN OWEN
who has wakened hope for many
in the darkness
of perfectionistic despair

Contents

WHEN THE DARKNESS WILL NOT LIFT

Doing What We Can
While We Wait for God–and Joy

I waited patiently for the LORD.

PSALM 40:1

Weeping may tarry for the night,
but joy comes with the morning.

PSALM 30:5

Ah my deare angrie Lord,
Since thou dost love, yet strike;
Cast down, yet help afford;
Sure I will do the like.

I will complain, yet praise;
I will bewail, approve:
And all my sowre-sweet dayes
I will lament, and love.

GEORGE HERBERT
"Bitter-sweet"[1]

---

[1] George Herbert, "Bitter-sweet," from his collection titled *The Temple* (1633), quoted from: http://www.ccel.org/h/herbert/temple/Bittersweet.html (accessed July 11, 2006).

Introduction

Faith Alone and the Fight for Joy

In addressing the topic of spiritual darkness, I am aware that I have put my oar in a very large sea. I rise from my desk and walk past a wall of books that speak more wisely than I on the care and cure of sad Christian souls. Just opening these volumes reminds me of how many wise and valuable things could be said— and cannot be said in a book of this size. It will always be so. The Word of God is inexhaustible, and the world he made holds countless treasures waiting to be found by clear eyes in search of Christ-exalting joy.

The needs of embattled people who fight for joy will always be as diverse as the people themselves. So I content myself with rowing out into this sea as far as my limits allow, and I pray that you will search out some of these great old books and go farther in your quest for joy than I am able to take you here.[1]

TO HELP THOSE FOR WHOM JOY STAYS OUT OF REACH

My aim is to give some guidance and hope to those for whom joy seems to stay out of reach. Virtually all Bible-saturated physicians of the soul have spoken about long seasons of darkness and desolation. In the old days they called it melancholy. Richard Baxter, for example, who died in 1691, wrote with astonishing relevance about the complexities of dealing with Christians who seem

---

[1] Willem Teellinck, *The Path of True Godliness*, trans. Annemie Godbehere, ed. Joel R. Beeke (repr. Grand Rapids, Mich: Baker, 2003); Richard Sibbes, *The Bruised Reed* (1630; repr. Edinburgh: Banner of Truth, 1998); William Bridge, *A Lifting Up for the Downcast* (1649; repr. Edinburgh: Banner of Truth, 1979); Jeremiah Burroughs, *The Rare Jewel of Christian Contentment* (1648; repr. Edinburgh: Banner of Truth, 1979); John Owen, *Overcoming Sin and Temptation* (Wheaton, Ill.: Crossway Books, 2006); John Owen, *Communion with God* (1657; repr. Edinburgh: Banner of Truth, 1992); Richard Baxter (died 1691), "The Cure of Melancholy and Overmuch Sorrow by Faith and Physic," in *Puritan Sermons 1659–1689*, vol. 3, ed. Samuel Annesley (Wheaton, Ill.: Richard Owen Roberts Publishers, 1981 [available to read at http://www.puritansermons.com/baxter/baxter25.htm]); Walter Marshall, *The Gospel Mystery of Sanctification* (1692; repr. Grand Rapids, Mich.: Reformation Heritage Books, 1999); Henry Scougal, *The Life of God in the Soul of Man* (1739; repr. Ross-shire, Scotland: Christian Focus, 1996); Jonathan Edwards, *The Religious Affections* (1746; repr. Edinburgh: Banner of Truth, 1986); Martyn Lloyd-Jones, *Spiritual Depression: Its Causes and Cures* (Grand Rapids: Eerdmans, 1965); Gaius Davies, *Genius, Grief and Grace: A Doctor Looks at Suffering and Success* (Ross-shire, Scotland: Christian Focus, 2001); J. I. Packer, *Faithfulness and Holiness: The Witness of J. C. Ryle* (Wheaton, Ill.: Crossway Books, 2002).

unable to enjoy God. "Delighting in God, and in his word and ways," he said, "is the flower and life of true religion. But these that I speak of can delight in nothing—neither God, nor in his word, nor any duty."[2]

I think that is technically an overstatement. At least I prefer to say that all true believers in Christ have within them the seed of joy, and that they do experience it in some real way. They may not have the "flower" of "true religion," but they do have the "life," even though it may be only a mustard seed of joy in Christ.[3] They have tasted and seen that the Lord Jesus is a sweet, life-giving spring of eternal joy for their souls (Ps. 34:8; 1 Pet. 2:2-3), but the taste, even though it indicates that there is true spiritual life, is easily overwhelmed by the floods of darkness that threaten to bury it. These are the ones I want to help in this small book.

THE FOUNDATION OF GUTSY GUILT

This book began as the final chapter of a larger book titled *When I Don't Desire God: How to Fight for Joy*.[4]

---

[2] Baxter, "The Cure of Melancholy," 257.

[3] For a fuller discussion of the relationship between joy and saving faith see John Piper, "The Purifying Power of Living by Faith" in *Future Grace* (Sisters, Oregon: Multnomah Publishers, 1995), chapters 14–16.

[4] John Piper, *When I Don't Desire God: How to Fight for Joy* (Wheaton: Crossway Books, 2004), 209-34.

I hope that if this small book proves helpful, readers will consider what is in the larger one. There are crucial foundations in that larger book which are not included here. One of the most important is learning to fight for joy like a justified sinner. I call this "gutsy guilt." Every embattled saint has learned this secret, even if they never called it by that name.

Gutsy guilt means learning to live on the rock-solid truth of what happened for us when Jesus Christ died on the cross and rose again from the dead. It means realizing that in this life we will always be sinful and imperfect. Therefore *in ourselves* we will always be guilty. This will prove emotionally devastating if we do not discover the reality of justification by faith, that is, the secret of gutsy guilt. This is not the only weapon with which we fight for joy in the darkness of discouragement, but it is one of the most foundational and the most important.

The biblical truth of justification says that my rescue from sin and God's wrath is first a legal rescue, and only then a moral one. First, I am legally absolved of guilt and credited with a righteousness that I don't have. That is, I am declared righteous in the courtroom of heaven, where God sits as judge, and where I, without justification, would stand condemned by his law. That's what the word "justify" means: not *make* just, but *declare* just.[5]

We can see this in Luke 7:29 where the people "justified *God*"! That is, they declared that he was just. They didn't *make* him just. The difference is that we are sinners and do not have a righteousness of our own. We should, but we don't. That's why we are guilty and destined for eternal punishment. This is the deepest root of all our misery. If we could sever this root, we would fight for joy as victors. God's gift of justification on the basis of Christ's blood and righteousness does sever this root of misery.

THE GREAT WORK OF CHRIST OUTSIDE OF US

To make a way for us to be saved, God sent Christ to live a perfect divine-human life, and die an obedient death. In this way Christ became both the substitute punishment for our sins (Matt. 26:28; 1 Cor. 15:3; 1 Pet. 3:18) and the substitute performer of our righteousness (Rom. 5:19; 10:4; 2 Cor. 5:21; Phil. 3:9). Therefore, in the courtroom

---

[5] For a fuller explanation and defense of this understanding of the doctrine of justification by faith, see John Piper, *Counted Righteous in Christ* (Wheaton: Crossway Books, 2002).

of God, my guilt for sin is removed by Christ's blood ("In him we have redemption through his blood, the forgiveness of our trespasses" [Eph. 1:7]); and my title to heaven is provided by Christ's obedience ("By the one man's obedience the many will be made righteous" [Rom. 5:19]). I am declared just—freed from the punishment of sin and now possessing a title to heaven. This is what the Bible means by justification.

The capstone of its joy-producing glory is that justification is *by faith alone* apart from works of the law. Paul said, "We hold that one is justified *by faith* apart from works of the law. . . . To the one who does not work but *trusts him who justifies the ungodly*, his faith is counted as righteousness" (Rom. 3:28; 4:4-5). The best news in all the world to the "ungodly," who grieve under the cloud of darkness and guilt, is the news that God, by faith alone, counts them as righteous because of Christ. This is the rock where we stand when the dark clouds gather and the floods lick at our feet: justification is by *grace alone* (not mixed with our merit), through *faith alone* (not mixed with our works) on the basis of Chri*st alone* (not mingling his righteousness with ours), to the glory of *God alone* (not ours).

CONFUSING JUSTIFICATION AND SANCTIFICATION WILL KILL JOY

Then, and only then, on the basis of this forgiveness and this declaration of righteousness, God gives us his Holy Spirit and progressively transforms us morally into the image of his Son. This progressive change is *not* justification, but is based on justification. This change is what we call *sanctification*. "Now that you have been set free from sin and have become slaves of God, the fruit you get leads to sanctification and its end, eternal life" (Rom. 6:22).

First, the legal issue is settled. In the courtroom of heaven, we ungodly sinners are declared righteous by faith alone. Christ's righteousness is imputed to us. We do not have a righteousness of our own when God accepts us. Our faith was not our righteousness. It was our desperate receiving of Christ and all that he is for us. We had not yet become loving. Instead, with empty hands we received Christ whose faithful life of love perfectly fulfilled the law of God. By faith alone we were united to Christ. And all that he is was imputed to us, the ungodly. This is justification. This is the settling of the legal issue first.

When that is settled—and it is settled in the twinkling of an eye—then the moral progress goes forward (sanctification) all too slowly, we lament. Both justification and sanctification are gifts from God. Both are bought by the blood of Christ. They are inseparable, but different. Both are by faith alone. Justification is by faith alone because only faith receives the declaration that we, the ungodly, are counted righteous. Sanctification is by faith alone because only faith receives the power to bear the fruit of love.

It is crucial in the fight for joy that we not confuse or combine justification and sanctification. Confusing them will, in the end, undermine the gospel, and turn justification by *faith* into justification by *performance*. If that happens, the great gospel weapon in the fight for joy will fall from our hands.

God accepts us on the basis of Christ's righteousness, not ours. To be sure, our progressive sanctification—our all-too-slow growth in Christlikeness—matters. It is the necessary evidence that the seed of spiritual life is in our soul and that our faith is real.[6] But,

---

[6] The historic *Westminster Confession of Faith* expresses well how faith alone justifies but is never alone, and always gives rise to love. "Those whom God effectually calleth He also freely justifieth; not by infusing righteousness into them, but by pardoning their sins, and by accounting and accepting their persons as righteous: not for anything wrought in them, or done by them, but for Christ's sake alone: nor by imputing faith itself, the act of believing, or any other evangelical obedience, to them as their righteousness; but by imputing the obedience and satisfaction of Christ unto them, they receiving and resting on Him and His righteousness, by faith: which faith they have not of themselves; it is the gift of God" (11.1); and "Faith, thus receiving and resting on Christ and His righteousness, is the alone instrument of justification; yet is it not alone in the person justified, but is ever accompanied with all other saving graces, and is no dead faith, but worketh by love" (11:2).

O what a difference it makes to be assured, in the discouraging darkness of our own imperfection, that we have a perfect righteousness *outside ourselves*, namely Christ's.

John Bunyan Sees His Righteousness in Heaven

This was John Bunyan's experience and he tells his story to encourage us to rejoice in the doctrine of justification—that there is a perfect, objective, external righteousness imputed to us that is not our own but Christ's. Bunyan is the one who wrote *The Pilgrim's Progress*, which has sold more copies in English than any book besides the Bible. He was a pastor in the seventeenth century who spent over twelve years in prison because he refused to stop preaching the word of the cross. The greatest Puritan theologian and contemporary of Bunyan, John Owen, when asked by King Charles why he went to hear an uneducated tinker preach, said, "I would willingly exchange my learning for the tinker's power of touching men's hearts."[7]

But Bunyan was not always so bold and full of

---

[7] John Brown, *John Bunyan: His Life, Times and Work* (London: The Hulbert Publishing Co., 1928), 366. This is a paraphrase of an indirect quote.

gospel power. In his twenties there were terrible strug-gles. "A whole flood of blasphemies, both against God, Christ, and the Scriptures were poured upon my spirit, to my great confusion and astonishment. . . . My heart was at times exceeding hard. If I would have given a thousand pounds for a tear, I could not shed one. . . . Oh, the desperateness of man's heart. . . . I feared that this wicked sin of mine might be that sin unpardon-able. . . . Oh, no one knows the terrors of those days but myself."[8]

Then came the decisive moment of triumph over despair and joylessness. It was an awakening to the magnificent truth of the imputation of Christ's righteousness.

> One day as I was passing into the field . . . this sentence fell upon my soul. *Thy righteousness is in heaven.* And . . . I saw with the eyes of my soul Jesus Christ at God's right hand; there, I say, was my righteousness; so that wherever I was, or whatever I was doing, God could not say of me, he [lacks] my righteousness, for that was just before him. I also saw, moreover, that it was not my good frame of heart that made my righteousness better, nor yet my bad frame that made my righteousness

---

[8] John Bunyan, *Grace Abounding to the Chief of Sinners* (Hertfordshire, England: Evangelical Press, 1978), 55-59.

worse, for my righteousness was Jesus Christ himself, "The same yesterday, today, and forever" (Heb. 13:8). Now did my chains fall off my legs indeed. I was loosed from my afflictions and irons; my temptations also fled away; so that from that time those dreadful scriptures of God [about the unforgivable sin] left off to trouble me; now went I also home rejoicing for the grace and love of God."[9]

START WITH DESPAIR IN YOURSELF

Bunyan went home rejoicing when he saw that his righteousness was outside himself. It was Jesus Christ. I pray that this will be your experience too. Where should you start? Start at the easiest place for those in darkness. Start with despair. Despair of finding any answer in yourself. I pray that you will cease from all efforts to look inside yourself for the rescue you need. I pray that you will do what only desperate people can do, namely, cast yourself on Christ. May you say to him, "You are my only hope. I have no righteousness in myself. I am overwhelmed with sin and guilt. I am under the wrath of God. My own conscience condemns me, and makes me miserable. I am perishing. Darkness is all about me. Have mercy upon me. I trust you."

---

[9] *Grace Abounding*, 90-91.

He has promised not to turn you away. "Whoever comes to me I will never cast out" (John 6:37). By this act of faith God will unite you to Jesus. You will be "in him," and in him you will be now and forever loved, forgiven, and righteous. The light will rise in your darkness in due time. God will hold onto you (Jude 24). You will make it. That is his promise: "Those whom he called he also justified, and those whom he justified he also glorified" (Rom. 8:30). The glory is coming. In the meantime, "this slight momentary affliction is preparing for us an eternal weight of glory beyond all comparison, as we look not to the things that are seen but to the things that are unseen. For the things that are seen are transient, but the things that are unseen are eternal." (2 Cor. 4:17-18).

1

The Darkness of Melancholy

How can we help Christians who seem unable to break out of darkness into the light of joy? Yes, I call them Christians, and thus assume that such things happen to genuine believers. It happens because of sin, or because of Satanic assault, or because of distressing circumstances, or because of hereditary or other physical causes. What makes the old books that I referred to in the Introduction so remarkable is the way they come to terms with all these causes and their many combinations, and how they address each condition appropriately. The old Puritan pastors never seemed to give up on anyone because of discouraging darkness.

Long before the rise of psychiatry and contemporary brain electrophysiology, Bible-saturated Puritan pastors recognized the complexity of causes behind the darkness of melancholy. In fact, the first answer Baxter mentions to the question, "What are the *causes* and *cure* of it?" is, "With very many there is a great part of the cause in distemper, weakness, and diseasedness of the body; and by it the soul is greatly disabled to any comfortable sense. But the more it ariseth from such natural necessity, it is the less sinful and less dangerous to the soul; but never the less troublesome."[1]

In his sermon on the causes and cures of melancholy, he has an entire section on "medicine and diet." He says, in his quaint but remarkably accurate language, "The disease called 'melancholy' is formally in the spirits, whose distemper unfits them for their office, in serving the imagination, understanding, memory, and affections; so by their distemper the thinking faculty is diseased, and becomes like an inflamed eye, or a foot

---

[1] Richard Baxter, "The Cure of Melancholy and Overmuch Sorrow by Faith and Physic," in *Puritan Sermons* 1659–1689, vol. 3, ed. Samuel Annesley (Wheaton, Ill.: Richard Owen Roberts Publishers, 1981 [available to read at *http://www.puritansermons.com/baxter/baxter25.htm*]), 258.

that is sprained or out of joint, disabled for its proper work."[2]

THE PHYSICAL SIDE OF SPIRITUAL DARKNESS

I will not go further in discussing the physical treatment of melancholy—and its severe form, depression. This is the work of a medical doctor, which I am not. What we should be clear about, though, is that the condition of our bodies makes a difference in the capacity of our minds to think clearly and of our souls to see the beauty of hope-giving truth. Martyn Lloyd-Jones, the great preacher at Westminster Chapel in London in the mid-twentieth century, began his helpful book *Spiritual Depression* by waving the flag of warning that we not overlook the physical. It is significant that Lloyd-Jones was a medical doctor before he was called to the ministry of preaching.

> Does someone hold the view that as long as you are a Christian it does not matter what the condition of your body is? Well, you will soon be disillusioned if you believe that. Physical conditions play their part in

---

[2] Ibid., 286.

all this. . . . There are certain physical ailments which tend to promote depression. . . . [T]ake that great preacher who preached in London for nearly forty years in the last century—Charles Haddon Spurgeon—one of the truly great preachers of all time. That great man was subject to spiritual depression, and the main explanation in his case was undoubtedly the fact that he suffered from a gouty condition which finally killed him. He had to face this problem of spiritual depression often in a most acute form. A tendency to acute depression is an unfailing accompaniment of the gout which he inherited from his forebears. And there are many, I find, who come to talk to me about these matters, in whose case it seems quite clear to me that the cause of the trouble is mainly physical. Into this group, speaking generally, you can put tiredness, overstrain, illness, any form of illness. You cannot isolate the spiritual from the physical for we are body, mind and spirit. The greatest and the best Christians when they are physically weak are more prone to an attack of spiritual depression than at any other time and there are great illustrations of this in the scriptures.[3]

Gaius Davies, a psychiatrist in Britain who knew Lloyd-Jones well, observed:

---

[3] Lloyd-Jones, *Spiritual Depression*, 18-19.

Before 1954, when the series of sermons on depression was completed, no effective antidepressant had been on the market, though some progress was made towards that in 1954. Later, in 1955-6 when new forms of medication were available freely, I know how concerned Dr. Lloyd-Jones was to know which kinds of antidepressants were most effective, because he asked me about them a good deal when I was beginning my medical career, and talked to other doctors in a similar way. He wanted to know enough to be able to advise those who asked his opinion.[4]

THE PLACE OF MEDICATION IN THE FIGHT FOR JOY

I do not want to give the impression that medication should be the first or main solution to spiritual darkness. Of course, by itself medicine is *never* a solution to *spiritual* darkness. All the fundamental issues of life remain to be brought into proper relation to Christ when the medicine has done its work. Antidepressants are not the decisive savior. Christ is. In fact, the almost automatic use of pills for child misbehavior and adult sorrows is probably going to hurt us as a society.

David Powlison, who edits *The Journal of Biblical*

---

[4] Davies, Genius, *Grief and Grace*, 354.

Counseling, counsels at the Christian Counseling and Educational Foundation, and lectures at Westminster Seminary, wrote of a sea change in the mental sciences in the mid-1990s:

> Have no doubt, the world did change in the mid-90s. The action is now in your body. It's what you got from Mom and Dad, not what they did to you. The *excitement* is about brain functions, not family dysfunctions. The *cutting edge* is in hard science medical research and psychiatry, not squishy soft, philosophy-of-life, feel-your-pain psychologies. . . . Biology is suddenly hot. Psychiatry has broken forth, a *blitzkrieg* sweeping away all opposition. . . . Medicine is poised to claim the human personality. . . . The biopsychologizing of human life is having a huge effect, both in culture and the church.[5]

His conclusion is that this preoccupation with biopsychiatry will pass, and as it does,

> biopsychiatry will cure a few things, for which we should praise the God of common grace. But in the long run, unwanted and unforeseen side effects will combine with vast disillusionment. The gains will never live up to the promises. And the lives of count-

---

[5] David Powlison, "Biological Psychiatry," in *Journal of Biblical Counseling* 17 (Spring 1999): 3-4.

less people, whose normal life problems are now being medicated, will not be qualitatively changed and redirected. Only intelligent repentance, living faith, and tangible obedience turn the world upside down.[6]

Powlison refers sympathetically to Ed Welch's book *Blame It on the Brain?* where Welch is willing to employ medication in cases of persistent debilitating depression. Welch says:

> If the person is not taking medication but is considering it, I typically suggest that he or she postpone that decision for a period of time. During that time, I consider possible causes, and together we ask God to teach us about both ourselves and him so that we can grow in faith in the midst of hardship. If the depression persists, I might let the person know that medication is an option to deal with some of the physical symptoms.[7]

To many, this may seem excessively cautious. But widespread scientific evidence is already reining in the initial enthusiasm about the unique effectiveness of

[6] Ibid., 6.
[7] Edward T. Welch, *Blame It on the Brain? Distinguishing Chemical Imbalances, Brain Disorders, and Disobedience* (Phillipsburg, N.J., P&R, 1998), 126.

antidepressants. One summary article in *The Washington Post* in May 2002 put the situation starkly like this:

> After thousands of studies, hundreds of millions of prescriptions and tens of billions of dollars in sales, two things are certain about pills that treat depression: Antidepressants like Prozac, Paxil and Zoloft work. And so do sugar pills. A new analysis has found that in the majority of trials conducted by drug companies in recent decades, sugar pills have done as well as—or better than—antidepressants.[8]

The point of Welch's caution and the *Post's* skepticism is not that depression or spiritual darkness is disconnected with our physical condition. They are deeply connected. The point is that the relationship between the soul and the brain is beyond human comprehension and should be handled with the greatest care and with profound attention to the moral and spiritual realities of human personhood that may exert as much influence on the brain as vice versa.

In other words, if someone reading this book is on

---

[8] Shankar Vedantam, "Against Depression, a Sugar Pill Is Hard to Beat," in *Washington Post* (May 7, 2002): A01. Cited from *www.washingtonpost.com/wp-dyn-articles/A42930-2002May6.html* (link defunct).

medication, or is thinking about it, I do not condemn you for that, nor does the Bible. It may or may not be the best course of action. I commend you to the wisdom of a God-centered, Bible-saturated medical doctor. If there was imperfection in the choice to use medication, the imputed righteousness of Christ will swallow it up as you rest in him.

2

WAITING IN DARKNESS, WE ARE NOT LOST AND NOT ALONE

With or without medication there are other things that can be done in the midst of prolonged darkness. And I would love to encourage you in some of these. It will be of great advantage to the struggling Christian to remember that seasons of darkness are normal in the Christian life. I don't mean that we should not try to live above them. I mean that if we do not succeed, we are not lost, and we are not alone, as the fragment of our faith cleaves to Christ. Consider the experience of David in Psalm 40:1-3:

> I waited patiently for the LORD;
> he inclined to me and heard my cry.
> He drew me up from the pit of destruction,
> out of the miry bog,
> and set my feet upon a rock,
> making my steps secure.
> He put a new song in my mouth,
> a song of praise to our God.
> Many will see and fear,
> and put their trust in the LORD.

The king of Israel is in "the pit of destruction" and "the miry bog"—descriptions of his spiritual condition. The song of praise is coming, he says, but it is not now on his lips. It is as if David had fallen into a deep, dark well and plunged into life-threatening mud. There was one other time when David wrote about this kind of experience. He combined the images of mud and flood: "Save me, O God! For the waters have come up to my neck. I sink in deep mire, where there is no foothold; I have come into deep waters, and the flood sweeps over me" (Ps. 69:1-2).

In this pit of mud and destruction there is a sense of helplessness and desperation. Suddenly air, just air, is worth a million dollars. Helplessness, desperation, apparent hopelessness, the breaking point for the over-worked businessman, the outer limits of exasperation for the mother of three constantly crying children, the impossible expectations of too many classes in school, the grinding stress of a lingering illness, the imminent attack of a powerful enemy. It is good that we don't know what the experience was. It makes it easier to see ourselves in the pit with the king. Anything that causes a sense of helplessness and desperation and threatens to ruin life or take it away—that is the king's pit.

How Long, O Lord, How Long!

Then comes the king's cry: "I waited patiently for the Lord; he inclined to me and heard my cry." One of the reasons God loved David so much was that he cried so much. "I am weary with my moaning; every night I flood my bed with tears; I drench my couch with my weeping" (Ps. 6:6). "You have kept count of my toss-ings; put my tears in your bottle. Are they not in your book?" (Ps. 56:8). Indeed they are! "Blessed are those who mourn" (Matt. 5:4). It is a beautiful thing when a broken man genuinely cries out to God.

Then after the cry you wait. "I waited patiently for the Lord." This is crucial to know: saints who cry to the

Lord for deliverance from pits of darkness must learn to wait patiently for the Lord. There is no statement about how long David waited. I have known saints who walked through eight years of debilitating depression and came out into glorious light. Only God knows how long we must wait. The prophet Micah experienced prolonged and painful waiting. "I sit in darkness . . . until [the Lord] pleads my cause and . . . will bring me out to the light" (Mic. 7:8-9). We can draw no deadlines for God. He hastens or he delays as he sees fit. And his timing is all-loving toward his children. Oh, that we might learn to be patient in the hour of darkness. I don't mean that we make peace with darkness. We fight for joy. But we fight as those who are saved by grace and held by Christ. We say with Paul Gerhardt that our night will soon—in God's good timing—turn to day:

> Give to the winds thy fears,
> Hope and be undismayed.
> God hears thy sighs and counts thy tears,
> God shall lift up thy head.
>
> Through waves and clouds and storms,
> He gently clears thy way;
> Wait thou His time; so shall this night
> Soon end in joyous day.

Far, far above thy thought,
His counsel shall appear,
When fully He the work hath wrought,
That caused thy needless fear.

Leave to His sovereign sway
To choose and to command;
So shalt thou, wondering, own that way,
How wise, how strong this hand.[1]

The Ground of Our Assurance When We Cannot See Our Faith[2]

It is utterly crucial that in our darkness we affirm the wise, strong hand of God to hold us, even when we have no strength to hold him. This is the way Paul thought of his own strivings. He said, "Not that I have already obtained this or am already perfect, but I press on to make it my own, because Christ Jesus has made me his own" (Phil. 3:12). The key thing to see in this verse is that all Paul's efforts to grasp the fullness of joy in Christ are secured by Christ's grasp of him. Never forget that your security rests on Christ's faithfulness first.

Our faith rises and falls. It has degrees. But our secu-

---

[1] Paul Gerhardt, "Give to the Winds Thy Fears" (1656), trans. John Wesley (1737), www.cyberhymnal.org/htm/g/i/givetotw.htm.
[2] For a biblical and balanced treatment of assurance, see Donald S. Whitney, *How Can I Be Sure I'm a Christian? What the Bible Says About Assurance of Salvation* (Colorado Springs: NavPress, 1994).

rity does not rise and fall. It has no degrees. We *must* persevere in faith. That's true. But there are times when our faith is the size of a mustard seed and barely visible. In fact, the darkest experience for the child of God is when his faith sinks out of his own sight. Not out of God's sight, but his. Yes, it is possible to be so overwhelmed with darkness that you do not know if you are a Christian—and yet still be one.

All the great doctors of the soul have distinguished between faith and its full assurance. The reason for this is that we are saved by the work of God causing us to be born again and bringing us to faith. "The wind blows where it wishes, and you hear its sound, but you do not know where it comes from or where it goes. So it is with everyone who is born of the Spirit" (John 3:8). We are not saved by producing faith on our own and then making that the basis of our new birth. It is the other way around, which means that God is at the bottom of my faith; and when it disappears for a season from my own view, God may yet be there sustaining its root in the new birth and protecting the seed from destruction. This was crucial in Richard Baxter's soul care.

> Certainty of our faith and sincerity is not necessary to salvation, but the sincerity of faith itself is necessary. He

shall be saved that giveth up himself to Christ, though he know not that he is sincere in doing it. Christ knoweth his own grace, when they that have it know not that it is sound.

An abundance are cast down by ignorance of themselves, not knowing the sincerity which God hath given them. Grace is weak in the best of us here; and little and weak grace is not very easily perceived, for it acteth weakly and unconstantly, and it is known but by its acts; and weak grace is always joined with too strong corruption; and all sin in heart and life is contrary to grace, and doth obscure it. . . . And how can any under all these hindrances, yet keep any full assurance of their own sincerity?[3]

Baxter's aim here is not to destroy a Christian's comfort. On the contrary, he wants to help us in the times of our darkness to know that we can be safe in Jesus, even when we have lost sight of our own sincerity. The witness of the Holy Spirit that we are the children of God (Rom. 8:16) may be clear or faint. But the reality is unshakable. "God's firm foundation stands, bearing this seal: 'The Lord knows those who are his'" (2 Tim. 2:19). "God is faithful, by whom you were called" (1 Cor. 1:9).

---

[3] Baxter, "The Cure of Melancholy," 266, 278.

"He who began a good work in you will bring it to completion at the day of Jesus Christ" (Phil. 1:6). Baxter's words are crucial counsel if we are to survive the dark night of the soul. And that night will come for almost every Christian. And when it comes, we must wait for the Lord, cry to him, and know that our own self-indictment, rendered in the darkness, is not as sure as God's Word spoken in the light.

WHEN A CHILD OF GOD IS PERSUADED THAT HE IS NOT

Christians in the darkness of depression may ask desperately, how can I know that I am truly a child of God? They are not usually asking to be reminded that we are saved by grace through faith. They know that. They are asking how they can know that their faith is real. God must guide us in how we answer, and knowing the person will help us know what to say.[4]

The first and best thing to say may be, "I love you. And I am not letting you go." In those words a person may feel God's keeping presence, which they may not

[4] For two helpful articles on depression and how to help those who struggle, see Edward T. Welch, "Counseling Those Who Are Depressed" and "Words of Hope for Those Who Struggle with Depression," *Journal of Biblical Counseling* 18, no. 2 (2000): 5-31, 40-46.

feel in any other way. Or, second, we might say, "Stop looking at your faith, and rivet your attention on Christ. Faith is sustained by looking at Christ, crucified and risen, not by turning from Christ to analyze your faith. Let me help you look to Christ. Let's read Luke 22 through 24 together." Paradoxically, if we would experience the joy of faith, we must not focus much on it. We must focus on the greatness of our Savior.

Third, we might call attention to the evidences of grace in their life. We might recount our own sense of their authenticity when we were loved by them, and then remind them of their own strong affirmations of the lordship of Christ. Then say, "No one can say 'Jesus is Lord' except in the Holy Spirit" (1 Cor. 12:3). This approach is not usually successful in the short run, because a depressed person is prone to discount all good assessments of his own condition; but it can be valuable in the long run, because it stands as an objective hope and act of love over against his own subjective darkness.

Fourth, we might remind the sufferer that his demand for a kind of absolute, mathematical certainty about his right standing with God is asking for too much. None of us lives with that kind of certainty about any relationships in life, and this need not destroy our comfort. As Baxter says, "No wife or child is certain that the husband or father will not murder them; and yet they may live comfortably, and not fear it."[5] In other words, there is a kind of certainty that we live by, and it is enough. It is, in the end, a gift of God.

One can imagine a wife obsessed with fear that her husband will kill her, or that during the night one of her children will kill another one. No amount of arguing may bring her away from the fear of this possibility. Rationally and mathematically it is possible. But millions of people live in complete peace about these things, even though there is no absolute $2 + 2 = 4$ kind of certainty. The certainty is rooted in good experience and the God-given stability of nature. It is a sweet assurance—and a gift of God. So we say to our suffering friend, "Don't demand the kind of certainty about your own relationship to God that you don't require about the other relationships in your life."

It follows from this that we should all fortify ourselves against the dark hours of depression by cultivating a deep distrust of the certainties of despair. Despair is relentless in the certainties of its pessimism. But we have seen again and again, from our own experience

---

[5] Baxter, "The Cure of Melancholy," 278.

and others', that absolute statements of hopelessness that we make in the dark are notoriously unreliable. Our dark certainties are not sureties. While we have the light, let us cultivate distrust of the certainties of despair.

3

FOLD NOT THE ARMS

OF ACTION

Waiting for the Lord in a season of darkness should not be a time of inactivity. We should do what we can do. And *doing* is often God's appointed remedy for despair. Wise Christian counselors, ancient and modern, have given this advice. George MacDonald, whom C. S. Lewis called "his master,"[1] wrote:

---

[1] C. S. Lewis, ed., *George MacDonald: An Anthology* (London: Geoffrey Bles, The Centenary Press, 1946), 20.

[God] changes not because thou changest. Nay, He has an especial tenderness of love towards thee for that thou art in the dark and hast no light, and His heart is glad when thou dost arise and say, "I will go to my Father." . . . Fold the arms of thy faith, and wait in the quietness until light goes up in thy darkness. Fold the arms of thy Faith I say, but not of thy Action: bethink thee of something that thou oughtest to do, and go to do it, if it be but the sweeping of a room, or the preparing of a meal, or a visit to a friend. Heed not thy feelings: Do thy work.[2]

Richard Baxter gave the same counsel three hundred years earlier than MacDonald and traced it back to the Bible.

Be sure that you live not idly, but in some constant business of a lawful calling, so far as you have bodily strength. Idleness is a constant sin, and labour is a duty. Idleness is but the devil's home for temptation, and for unprofitable, distracting musings. Labour profiteth others and ourselves; both soul and body need it. Six days must thou labour, and must not eat "The bread of idleness." (Prov. xxxi. 13-27.) God hath made it our duty, and will bless us in his appointed way. I have known grievous, despairing melancholy cured and turned into

---

[2] Ibid., 36. See the quote in its context from the sermon "The Eloi," at *http://www.johannesen.com/SermonsSeriesI.htm.*

a life of godly cheerfulness, principally by setting upon
constancy and diligence in the business of families and
callings.[3]

WHAT MATTERS IS YOUR DUTY, NOT YOUR JOY?

This counsel from MacDonald and Baxter raises a crit-
ical question. They both seem to make feelings negligi-
ble. They seem to say: What matters is that you do your
duty, not that you feel joy. But that may not be what
they mean, and if it were, I would strongly disagree.
When MacDonald says, "Heed not thy feelings: Do thy
work," he means: don't let *wrong* feelings govern you.
Act against them. If your feelings are telling you that
staying in bed is the best thing today, preach to your
feelings and tell them how foolish they are. Don't lose
sight of the gospel in this preaching! Don't forget that
defeating these wrong feelings and getting out of bed is
enabled by the Spirit and is *becoming what you are in
Christ*. But then exert your will and get up! I certainly
agree with this.

But the question is deeper: If joy in God is the foun-

[3] Baxter, "The Cure of Melancholy," 282.

tain of love and the root of right living—as I believe it is—can behavior that proceeds without joy be virtuous? I will answer the question at two levels.

First, I would say that a Christian, no matter how dark the season of his sadness, never is completely without joy in God. I mean that there remains in his heart the seed of joy in the form, perhaps, of only a remembered taste of goodness and an unwillingness to let the goodness go. This is not the "joy that is inexpressible and filled with glory" (1 Pet. 1:8). It's not the joy that we have known at times and fight to regain. But it is a fragment of such joy—like a man who sits in prison and pulls out a tattered picture of his wife, or a paralyzed victim of a car accident who watches a video of the day he could dance. Or, even more fragmentary, the joy may only lie there in the cellar of our soul in the form of penitent sadness that we cannot desire God as we ought. Inside that sadness is the seed of what we once knew of joy.

DUTY INCLUDES THE DUTY OF JOY

The other answer I would give is that we should never say to ourselves or another person in the season of darkness, "Just do your work. Just do your duty. Just act like a Christian, even if you don't feel like one." That's almost good advice. But the problem is in the word *just*. Instead of only saying, "Just do your duty," we must say four other things as well.

First, we must say that joy is part of your duty. The Bible says, "Rejoice always" (1 Thess. 5:16). And in regard to the duty of giving, it says, "God loves a *cheerful* giver" (2 Cor. 9:7). In regard to the duty of service, it says, "Serve the Lord *with gladness*" (Ps. 100:2). In regard to the duty of mercy, it says do it "*with cheerfulness*" (Rom. 12:8). In regard to the duty of afflictions, it says, "*Count it all joy*" (James 1:2). We simply water down the divine command when we call someone to half their duty.

The second thing we must say when we tell a disconsolate person to "do their job" is that while they do their job, they should probably be repenting and confessing the sin of gloomy faith. I say "probably" because even in cases where the main cause is physical, there is probably some element of sinful pride or self-pity mingled with it. I am aware that this may sound like an added burden to the one who is in spiritual darkness. But it is not an *added* burden. If it is a burden at all, it is already there and not *added* by calling it what it is.

Failing to rejoice in God when we are commanded to rejoice is sin. False comforts lead to artificial healing. But the truest diagnoses lead to the deepest cures. So, yes, we tell the disconsolate: "If you can, get up from your bed and make a meal, or sweep a room, or take a walk, or visit a friend, or go to work. But it is not a matter of indifference whether you do this with joy in God, and if you can't, then tell him so, and that you are sorry. He will hear you mercifully and forgive."

WILL YOU BE A HYPOCRITE IF YOU OBEY WITHOUT JOY?

Which leads to the third thing we say along with "Do your duty." We say: As you are able to do some of your duty, ask God that the joy be restored. That is, don't sit and wait for the joy, saying, "I will be a hypocrite if I do an act of mercy today, since I do not feel the joy of mercy." No, you will not be a hypocrite, *if* you know that joy is your duty, and repent that you don't have it, and ask God earnestly to restore the joy even as you do the deed. That is *not* the way a hypocrite thinks. That is the way a true Christian thinks in the fight for joy.

And the fourth thing we say, when we counsel the depressed Christian to be up and doing something good, is, "Be sure to thank God as you work that he has given you at least the will to work." Do not say, "But it is hypocritical to thank God with my tongue when I don't *feel* thankful in my heart." There is such a thing as hypocritical thanksgiving. Its aim is to conceal ingratitude and get the praise of men. That is not your aim. Your aim in loosing your tongue with words of gratitude is that God would be merciful and fill your *words* with the *emotion* of true gratitude. You are not seeking the praise of men; you are seeking the mercy of God. You are not hiding the hardness of ingratitude, but hoping for the inbreaking of the Spirit.

Thanksgiving with the Mouth Stirs Up Thankfulness in the Heart

Moreover, we should probably ask the despairing saint, "Do you know your heart so well that you are sure the words of thanks have no trace of gratitude in them?" I, for one, distrust my own assessment of my motives. I doubt that I know my good ones well enough to see all the traces of contamination. And I doubt that I know my bad ones well enough to see the traces of grace. Therefore, it is not folly for a Christian to assume that there is a residue of gratitude in his heart when he speaks and sings of God's goodness even though he feels little or nothing.

To this should be added that experience shows that *doing* the right thing, in the way I have described, is often the way toward *being* in the right frame. Hence Baxter gives this wise counsel to the oppressed Christian:

> Resolve to spend most of your time in thanksgiving and praising God. If you cannot do it with the joy that you should, yet do it as you can. You have not the power of your comforts: but have you no power of your tongues? Say not, that you are unfit for thanks and praises unless you have a praising heart and were the children of God: for every man, good and bad, is bound to praise God, and to be thankful for all that he hath received, and to do it as well as he can, rather than leave it undone. . . . Doing it as you can is the way to be able to do it better. Thanksgiving stirreth up thankfulness in the heart.[4]

---

[4] Ibid., 281.

4

DOES UNCONFESSED SIN CLOG OUR JOY?

It may be that part of the cause of spiritual darkness is cherished sin that we are unwilling to let go. I have assumed so far in this book that the pursuit of joy implies hatred for sin. Sin destroys joy. It offers deceptive delights, but it kills in the end. In dealing with our sin we can make two mistakes. One is to make light of it. The other is to be overwhelmed by it. In the fight for joy we must take it seriously, hate it, renounce it, and trust Christ as our only Savior from its guilt and power.

One of the reasons that some people suffer from

extended times of darkness is the unwillingness to renounce some cherished sin. Jesus and the Apostle Peter and King David all spoke of how unconfessed sin hinders our joy in God. Jesus said, "If you are offering your gift at the altar and there remember that your brother has something against you, leave your gift there before the altar and go. First be reconciled to your brother, and then come and offer your gift" (Matt. 5:23-24). We quench the joy of fellowship with God when we refuse to confess our offenses to man. Peter related this to marriage and said that if a husband sins against his wife, his prayers will be hindered (1 Pet. 3:7). If we want the joy of seeing and savoring God in Christ, we must not make peace with our sins. We must make war.

Listen to the experience of David that comes from unconfessed and unforsaken sin in his life: "Blessed is the man against whom the LORD counts no iniquity, and in whose spirit there is no deceit. For *when I kept silent, my bones wasted away through my groaning* all day long" (Ps. 32:2-3). These words are full of hope. We can hold fast to our sin, keep it secret, and "groan all day long" in darkness—or we can confess it and experience the stunning experience of "the man against whom the Lord counts no iniquity."

The almost incredible hope of confessing and renouncing sin is that the Lord does not then rub it in our face but cancels it. He does not count it against us. From this side of Calvary, we know how God can do that with justice. Christ bore the wrath of God for that sin (Gal. 3:13). We don't have to. The accounts are settled. Therefore, we should not fear to confess and let go of any cherished sin. The shame will not haunt us. Christ clothes us with his own righteousness (2 Cor. 5:21).

CONFESSING TO GOD AND TO MAN IS SWEET FREEDOM

As we ponder both the deep, unconscious depravity of our souls and the presumptuous sins of our wills, we should pray the words of Psalm 19:12-13: "Who can discern his errors? Declare me innocent from hidden faults. Keep back your servant also from presumptuous sins; let them not have dominion over me!" We have *hidden* faults that we cannot even confess, because we don't know what they are. And we have sins that we know about. It is good news to realize there is a biblical prayer that covers both. "Declare me innocent" of the ones I don't know about (because of Christ's blood), and "keep back your servant" from the ones I do know about (by Christ's power). If you hold fast to sin instead of renouncing it and fighting it, the darkness will remain as a severe but merciful witness to the outcome of cherishing idols.

Do not be content with whispering your sin to God. That is good. Very good. But he offers us something more: "Confess your sins *to one another* and pray for one another, that you may be healed" (James 5:16). There is a release and healing that flows from confessing not only to God in the secret place of your heart, but also to a trusted friend, or to the person you have offended. The tender words, "I'm sorry, will you forgive me?" are one of the surest paths to joy.

GIVE THE DEVIL HIS DUE, BUT NO MORE

If you ask about the devil's role in your darkness, I answer: give him his due, but no more. He and his demons are *always* at work, not just sometimes. There is nothing extraordinary about the *fact* of his harassment. Paul considers it a normal part of Christian warfare to "take up the shield of faith, with which you can extinguish all the flaming darts of the evil one" (Eph. 6:16). Peter counsels us, "Be sober-minded; be watchful. Your adversary the devil prowls around like a roaring lion, seeking someone to devour. Resist him, firm in your faith" (1 Pet. 5:8-9). All this is normal. But the quality of his harassment varies from mild temptation to murder. Jesus calls him "a murderer from the beginning" (John 8:44). He has the power to inspire painful persecution and even kill Christians (Rev. 2:10).

But there are three great comforts in the face of Satan's attacks. One is that Satan cannot do anything apart from God's sovereign permission (Job 1:12; 2:6), which is governed by God's infinite wisdom and covenant love. Thus Satan's servants become God's sanctifying envoys (2 Cor. 12:7-10). So even if Satan has a hand in your darkness, he is not free to do more than your loving Father permits, and God will turn it for your good (Luke 22:31-32).

Second, the decisive blow against Satan's destructive power was delivered by the death of Jesus for our sins (Col. 2:15; Heb. 2:14). This means that Satan can harass us and even kill us, but he cannot destroy us. Only unforgiven sin can damn the human soul. If Christ has covered all our sin by his blood, and if God imputes to us the perfect righteousness of Christ, then Satan has no grounds for any damning accusation, and his case against us fails in the court of heaven. "Who shall bring any charge against God's elect? It is God who justifies. Who is to condemn? Christ Jesus is the one who died" (Rom. 8:33-34).

THE DEVIL CANNOT ABIDE WITH THE LIGHT OF CHERISHED TRUTH

Third, deliverance from Satan's oppressing, darkening, and deceiving work in the life of the Christian comes most often by the power of truth, and only rarely by exorcism. I have seen demon-possession and have been a part of one very dramatic exorcism. I don't believe the person was a Christian till after the deliverance. The complete takeover of the personality by a demon is not something the Holy Spirit would allow in the Christ-indwelt heart. But that distinction may not matter much to the Christian who is being attacked and harassed from without on every side. The battle can be fierce. What is called for usually is the ministry of 2 Timothy 2:24-26:

> The Lord's servant must not be quarrelsome but kind to everyone, able to teach, patiently enduring evil, cor-recting his opponents with gentleness. God may per-haps grant them repentance leading to a knowledge of

the truth, and they may escape from the snare of the devil, after being captured by him to do his will.

Gentle, loving, teaching of the *truth*—especially the truth of the *gospel* of Jesus' death and resurrection for our deliverance from sin and wrath and death and Satan—is the process in which God himself grants repentance and a knowledge of the *truth*, which results in an escape from the captivity of the devil. The devil cannot abide truth and light. He is by nature a liar and deceiver. He thrives in darkness. Therefore, if by God's grace we can bring the full force of truth to shine in the believer's darkness, the devil will not survive the light. Good, solid Bible teaching is a crucial part of deliverance from the darkening power of the devil.[1]

---

[1] For a careful and wise biblical assessment of the devil's role in the Christian life and how Jesus and we should make war, see David Powlison, *Power Encounters: Reclaiming Spiritual Warfare* (Grand Rapids, Mich.: Baker, 1995).

5

THE DARKNESS
THAT FEEDS ON
SELF-ABSORPTION

S ometimes the darkness of our souls is owing in part to the fact that we have drifted into patterns of life that are not blatantly sinful but are constricted and uncaring. Our world has shrunk down to mere prudential concerns about ourselves and our families. Ethics has diminished from global concerns of justice and mercy and missions down to little lists of bad things to avoid. We find ourselves not energized for any great cause, but always thinking about the way to maximize our leisure and escape pressure. Unconsciously we have become very self-absorbed and oblivious and uncaring toward the pain and suffering in the world that is far worse than our own.

Paradoxically, depressed persons may say that they must care for themselves and cannot take on the problems of the world, when in fact part of the truth may be that their depression is feeding on the ingrown quality of their lives. This hit home to me when Bill Leslie came to Minneapolis some years ago and told his story. Bill Leslie was the pastor of LaSalle Street Church in Chicago, Illinois, from 1961 to 1989. He died of a heart attack at the age of sixty-one in 1993. His ministry was marked by concern for the whole person in the context of Chicago urban life. In an article on "Compassionate Evangelicalism," *Christianity Today* listed Leslie among the "early holistic ministry leaders."[1]

How Bill Leslie Became a Watered Garden and a Spring

He told of a near breakdown that he had, and how a spiritual mentor directed him to Isaiah 58. He said it

---

[1] Joel Carpenter, "Compassionate Evangelicalism," *Christianity Today* (December 2003), http://www.Christianitytoday.com/ct/2003/012/2.40.html (accessed July 11, 2006).

was verses 10-11 that rescued him from a season of darkness marked by feelings of exhaustion, burnout, and a dead-end ministry. The text says:

> If you pour yourself out for the hungry and satisfy the desire of the afflicted, then shall your light rise in the darkness and your gloom be as the noonday. And the LORD will guide you continually and satisfy your desire in scorched places and make your bones strong; and you shall be like a watered garden, like a spring of water, whose waters do not fail.

What struck Pastor Leslie so powerfully was the fact that if we pour ourselves out for others, God promises to make us like "a watered garden"—that is, we will receive the water we need for refreshment and joy. But even more, we will thus be "a spring of water" that does not fail—for others, for the demanding, exhausting, draining ministry of urban self-giving. He saw that God's way of lifting gloom and turning it into light was to "pour yourself out for the hungry and satisfy the desire of the afflicted." This gave him a pattern of divine life that got him through his crisis and kept him going for the rest of his days.

God has made us to flourish by being spent for others. Jesus said, "It is more blessed to give than to receive" (Acts 20:35). Most of us do not *choose* against this life of outpouring; we *drift* away from it. We confuse pressured family life and stresses at work with Christian sacrifice, when in fact much of it has little to do with meeting the needs of the hungry and afflicted and perishing.

Please hear me carefully. This is not the diagnosis for all depression or discouragement. If it were, such self-giving servants would never be depressed. But they are. My point is that *one* of the causes of some people's darkness is a slowly creeping self-absorption and small-mindedness. And the cure may be the gradual embrace of a vision of life that is far greater than our present concerns. Some things may have to be taken out of our schedule. But as health and joy return, we may be capable of more than we ever dreamed.

What My Eighty-Five-Year-Old Father Said Was Missing

I would mention in particular the life-giving, joy-producing effect of sharing your faith with unbelievers by word and deed. While writing the first draft of this book, I called my eighty-five-year-old father and said, "Daddy, I am writing a book on how to fight for joy.

What one thing comes to your mind from sixty years of ministry as to what Christians could do to increase their joy?" Almost without hesitation he said, "Share their faith." Joy in Christ thrives on being shared. That is the essence of Christian joy: It overflows or dies.

Millions of Christians live with a low-grade feeling of guilt for not openly commending Christ by their words. They try to persuade themselves that keeping their noses morally clean is a witness to Christ. The problem with this notion is that millions of unbelievers keep their noses morally clean. Christians will—and should—continue to feel bad for not sharing their faith. Christ is the most glorious person in the world. His salvation is infinitely valuable. Everyone in the world needs it. Horrific consequences await those who do not believe on Jesus. By grace alone we have seen him, believed on him, and now love him. Therefore, not to speak of Christ to unbelievers, and not to care about our city or the unreached peoples of the world is so contradictory to Christ's worth, people's plight, and our joy that it sends the quiet message to our souls day after day: This Savior and this salvation do not mean to you what you say they do. To maintain great joy in Christ in the face of that persistent message is impossible.

THE AIM IS THAT OUR WORDS WOULD BE THE OVERFLOW OF JOY IN CHRIST

I am aware, again, that this will feel like added guilt for the depressed person. It is not added. It is already there. Hiding it is like hiding part of the diagnosis of a person's disease. Jesus said shocking things, and hiding them will serve no one well in the long run. "Everyone who acknowledges me before men, I also will acknowledge before my Father who is in heaven, but whoever denies me before men, I also will deny before my Father who is in heaven" (Matt. 10:32-33). This is not meant by Jesus as a heavy burden or a hard yoke. "Come to me, all who labor and are heavy laden, and I will give you rest. Take my yoke upon you, and learn from me, for I am gentle and lowly in heart, and you will find rest for your souls. For my yoke is easy, and my burden is light" (Matt. 11:28-30).

What makes the gospel good news is not that Christ can be buried in our TV-saturated lives without the loss of joy. What makes it good news is that God is long-suffering and willing to forgive and start over with us again and again. The depressed person cannot simply go out and proclaim the joy of the Lord. But little by little a life can be built on grace and forgiveness that comes to the point where to be an advocate and a witness to Jesus is like breathing—and just as life-giving. The fight is to enjoy Christ so much that speaking of him is the overflow and increase of that enjoyment.[2]

Is the Cause You Live for Large Enough for Your Christ-exalting Heart?

J. Campbell White, secretary of the Laymen's Missionary Movement, said in 1909:

> Most men are not satisfied with the permanent output of their lives. Nothing can wholly satisfy the life of Christ within his followers except the adoption of Christ's purpose toward the world he came to redeem. Fame, pleasure and riches are but husks and ashes in contrast with the boundless and abiding joy of working with God for the fulfillment of his eternal plans. The men who are putting everything into Christ's undertaking are getting out of life its sweetest and most priceless rewards.[3]

---

[2] For biblical and encouraging help in personal evangelism, see Will Metzger, *Tell the Truth: The Whole Gospel to the Whole Person by Whole People*, revised and expanded edition (Downers Grove, Ill.: InterVarsity Press, 2002).

[3] J. Campbell White, "The Laymen's Missionary Movement," in *Perspectives on the World Christian Movement*, ed. Ralph D. Winter and Steven C. Hawthorne (Pasadena, Calif.: William Carey Library, 1981), 222.

In the midst of darkness, saints may have no strength to pursue such global dreams. But it may be, in the mercy of God, that as we wait for the light to go up, we can do poorly what we would love to do well. Perhaps we can read a short article about the church in China. Or listen to a tape about a missionary who suffered much for the gospel. Or write a note to a missionary family with a few lines about how we are hanging onto grace, and include a brief prayer for them.

6

LOVING THOSE WHO
CANNOT SEE THE LIGHT

For most people who are passing through the dark night of the soul, the turnaround will come because God brings unwavering lovers of Christ into their lives who do not give up on them. Throughout Richard Baxter's sermon on the causes and cures of melancholy are strewn counsels to the church on how to carry the burdens of the depressed. He says things like, "Often set before them the great truths of the gospel which are fittest to comfort them; and read them informing, comforting books; and live in a loving, cheerful manner with them."[1] If depressed saints cannot read the Bible or a good book, we should read it to them.

THE AMAZING GRACE OF JOHN NEWTON'S CARE FOR COWPER

One great example of persevering love for a depressed friend is John Newton,[2] the English pastor who wrote "Amazing Grace." He was one of the healthiest, happiest pastors in the eighteenth century. This proved to be life-giving—to a point—for a suicidal poet named William Cowper, who wrote some of our best-known hymns. Newton had drunk deeply at the fountain of grace, the cross of Jesus Christ. He was filled with joy and overflowing for those who weren't. To taste the kind of person Newton was, listen to this testimony he wrote about how he lived his days.

---

[1] Richard Baxter, "The Cure of Melancholy," 284.

[2] For the fuller story of Cowper and Newton from which this material is taken see John Piper, "The Clouds Ye So Much Dread Are Big with Mercy': Insanity and Spiritual Songs in the Life of William Cowper," in *The Hidden Smile of God: The Fruit of Affliction in the Lives of John Bunyan, William Cowper, and David Brainerd* (Wheaton, Ill.: Crossway Books, 2001), 81-122. For more on Newton, see John Piper, "John Newton: The Tough Roots of His Habitual Tenderness," in *The Roots of Endurance: Invincible Perseverance in the Lives of John Newton, Charles Simeon, and William Wilberforce* (Wheaton, Ill.: Crossway Books, 2002), 41-75.

Two heaps of human happiness and misery; now if I can take but the smallest bit from one heap and add to the other, I carry a point. If, as I go home, a child has dropped a halfpenny, and if, by giving it another, I can wipe away its tears, I feel I have done something. I should be glad to do greater things, but I will not neglect this. When I hear a knock on my study door, I hear a message from God; it may be a lesson of instruction; perhaps a lesson of penitence; but, since it is his message, it must be interesting.[3]

In 1767, at the age of thirty-six, William Cowper entered Newton's life while Newton was pastor at Olney. Cowper had already had a total mental breakdown and had attempted suicide three different times. He had been institutionalized at St. Alban's Insane Asylum, where God met him in a powerful way through the loving care of Dr. Nathaniel Cotton, and by a converting encounter with the gospel in Romans 3:25.

Immediately I received the strength to believe it, and the full beams of the Sun of Righteousness shone upon me. I saw the sufficiency of the atonement He had made, my pardon sealed in His blood, and all the fullness and

---

[3] Gilbert Thomas, *William Cowper and the Eighteenth Century* (London: Ivor Nicholson and Watson, Ltd., 1935), 202.

completeness of His justification. In a moment I believed, and received the gospel.[4]

After his release from St. Alban's, Cowper moved in with the Unwin family in a parish near Olney. When the father of the family died, Newton came to console them. Cowper was so helped by what he heard that he and Mrs. Unwin moved to Olney to be a part of Newton's church. For the next thirteen years Newton tended the tangled garden of Cowper's soul. Cowper said, "A sincerer or more affectionate friend no man ever had."[5]

While there, Cowper entered a time of spiritual despair that made him feel utterly God-forsaken and lost. This lasted most of the rest of his life until he died in 1800. Again there were repeated attempts at suicide, and each time God providentially prevented him. Newton stood by him all the way through this, even sacrificing at least one vacation so as not to leave Cowper alone.

In 1780, Newton left Olney for a new pastorate in London, where he served for the next twenty-seven

[4] Ibid., 132.
[5] Ibid., 192.

years. It is a great tribute to him that he did not abandon his friendship with Cowper, though this would, no doubt, have been emotionally easy to do. Instead, there was an earnest exchange of letters for twenty years. Cowper poured out his soul to Newton as he did to no one else.

The last days of Cowper's life brought no relief. There was no happy ending. In March 1800, Cowper said to the visiting doctor, "I feel unutterable despair." On April 24, Miss Perowne offered some refreshment to him, to which he replied, "What can it signify?" He never spoke again and died the next afternoon.[6]

To the end Newton remained Cowper's pastor and friend, writing and visiting him again and again. He did not despair of the despairing. After one of these visits in 1788 Cowper wrote,

> I found those comforts in your visit, which have formerly
> sweetened all our interviews, in part restored. I knew
> you; knew you for the same shepherd who was sent to
> lead me out of the wilderness into the pasture where the
> Chief Shepherd feeds His flock, and felt my sentiments of
> affectionate friendship for you the same as ever.[7]

---

[6] Ibid., 384.
[7] Ibid., 356.

THERE IS NO WASTED WORK IN LOVING THOSE WITHOUT LIGHT

You cannot persuade a depressed person that he has not been utterly rejected by God if he is persuaded that he has been. But you can stand by him. And you can keep soaking him, as Newton did for Cowper, in the "benevolence, mercy, goodness, and sympathy" of Jesus, and "the sufficiency of the atonement," and "the fullness and completeness of Christ's justification."[8] He may say that the comforts of Christ are wonderful but do not belong to him—as Cowper did. But in God's time these truths may yet be given the power to awaken hope and beget a spirit of adoption. Or, even in the absence of evidence that peace is given, they may be used in some mysterious way to sustain the mustard seed of faith that is so small it cannot be seen.

I do not know with certainty the outcome of Cowper's fight for joy. But I do know that true saints enter dark seasons, and should they die in the midst of one, it is no sure sign that they were not born again, nor that they were not sustained in their darkness by the

---

[8] Ibid., 131-32.

sovereign hand of grace. God has his reasons why he would leave one of his dear children feeling so forsaken. Indeed he left his own precious Son forsaken on the cross—"My God, my God, why have you forsaken me?" (Matt. 27:46). And we know his reasons were full of love for him and for us.

God has his reasons, even for the martyrdom of his closest friends. Peter is the clearest example. After Jesus' resurrection he said to Peter, "'Truly, truly, I say to you, when you were young, you used to dress yourself and walk wherever you wanted, but when you are old, you will stretch out your hands, and another will dress you and carry you where you do not want to go.' (*This he said to show by what kind of death he was to glorify God.*) And after saying this he said to him, 'Follow me.'" (John 21:18-19). In other words, Jesus said that Peter will die, it appears by crucifixion ("you will stretch out your hands"), and it will not be in vain. It will be for the glory of God.

But often we cannot see the more detailed reasons why God appoints for us a season of darkness and suffering. Gaius Davies tells the following story:

Winston Churchill used to speak of his "black dog": he survived though he was dogged by depression for much of his life. It is said that only because Churchill had faced his own black periods was he able, at sixty years of age, to rally those who felt overwhelmed by the Nazi threat. His own experience of adversity enabled him to be a leader who helped to save the world from the darkness of tyranny.[9]

But Cowper did not live to lead a nation into triumphant war. He died miserable. What was his "black dog" good for? It is not for us to render this final judgment. But I bear one small testimony. Without his struggles he probably would not have written "There Is a Fountain Filled with Blood" and brought hope to thousands of sinners who fear they have sinned their lives away:

> The dying thief rejoiced to see that fountain in his
> day;
> And there have I, though vile as he, washed all my
> sins away.
> Washed all my sins away, washed all my sins away;
> And there have I, though vile as he, washed all my
> sins away.[10]

---

[9] Davies, *Genius, Grief and Grace*, 13.
[10] William Cowper, "There Is a Fountain Filled with Blood" (1772).

And he would not have written "God Moves in a Mysterious Way" and by it helped me and many others through a hundred thickets of discouragement.

> God moves in a mysterious way
> His wonders to perform;
> He plants his footsteps in the sea
> And rides upon the storm.
>
> Deep in unfathomable mines
> Of never failing skill
> He treasures up his bright designs
> And works his sovereign will.
>
> You fearful saints, fresh courage take;
> The clouds you so much dread
> Are big with mercy and shall break
> In blessings on your head.
>
> His purposes will ripen fast,
> Unfolding every hour;
> The bud may have a bitter taste,
> But sweet will be the flower.
>
> Blind unbelief is sure to err
> And scan his work in vain;
> God is his own interpreter,
> And he will make it plain.[11]

---

[11] William Cowper, "God Moves in a Mysterious Way" (1774).

There is a legacy of severe mercy in writings such as these. The words are costly. And so they prove precious. So it is with everyone who stands beside a melancholy saint and helps him fight for joy.

William Cowper testified that the legacy had been left to him by another embattled poet and pastor, George Herbert, who had died at the age of thirty-nine in 1633. Cowper said, "This was the only author I had any delight reading. I pored over him all day long; and though I found not here what I might have found—a cure for my malady, yet it never seemed so much alleviated as while I was reading him."[12] Not surprisingly, therefore, a poem by Herbert wonderfully sums up this chapter and this book. It's called "Bitter-sweet." I hope you will read it twice, once to get the flow, and once aloud (as poetry is meant to be read) for the beauty and the meaning. Please don't stumble over the old-fashioned spelling. Herbert would be very happy if you were encouraged in your fight for joy.

> Ah my deare angrie Lord,
> Since thou dost love, yet strike;
> Cast down, yet help afford;
> Sure I will do the like.

---

[12] Davies, *Genius, Grief and Grace*, 103-4.

I will complain, yet praise;
I will bewail, approve:
And all my sowre-sweet dayes
I will lament, and love.[13]

Or as the apostle Paul put it for all the saints who fight for joy in this fallen world of pain and suffering, we live and minister "as sorrowful, yet always rejoicing" (2 Cor. 6:10).

---

[13] Herbert, "Bitter-sweet."

⚓ desiringGod

If you would like to further explore the vision of God and life presented in this book, we at Desiring God would love to serve you. We have hundreds of resources to help you grow in your passion for Jesus Christ and help you spread that passion to others. At our website, desiringGod.org, you'll find almost everything John Piper has written and preached, including more than thirty books. We've made over twenty-five years of his sermons available free online for you to read, listen to, download, and in some cases watch.

In addition, you can access hundreds of articles, listen to our daily internet radio program, find out where John Piper is speaking, learn about our conferences, discover our God-centered children's curricula, and browse our online store. John Piper receives no royalties from the books he writes and no compensation from Desiring God. The funds are all reinvested into our gospel-spreading efforts. DG also has a whatever-you-can-afford policy, designed for individuals with limited discretionary funds. If you'd like more information about this policy, please contact us at the address or phone number below. We exist to help you treasure Jesus Christ and his gospel above all things because he is most glorified in you when you are most satisfied in him. Let us know how we can serve you.

Desiring God
2601 East Franklin Avenue
Minneapolis, MN 55406

888.346.4700 (TELEPHONE)
612.338.4372 (FAX)
mail@desiringGod.org (EMAIL)
www.desiringGod.org (WEB)